Anonymous

Designs from Greek vases in the British museum

Anonymous

Designs from Greek vases in the British museum

ISBN/EAN: 9783337730741

Printed in Europe, USA, Canada, Australia, Japan

Cover: Foto ©ninafisch / pixelio.de

More available books at **www.hansebooks.com**

DESIGNS

FROM

GREEK VASES

IN THE

BRITISH MUSEUM

Edited by A. S. MURRAY

Keeper of Greek and Roman Antiquities

LONDON:

PRINTED BY ORDER OF THE TRUSTEES

AND SOLD AT THE MUSEUM

AND BY LONGMANS AND CO., 39 PATERNOSTER ROW

B. QUARITCH, 15 PICCADILLY; ASHER AND CO., 13 BEDFORD STREET, COVENT GARDEN

KEGAN PAUL, TRENCH, TRÜBNER AND CO., CHARING CROSS ROAD

AND THE OXFORD UNIVERSITY PRESS, AMEN CORNER

1894

LONDON :
PRINTED BY WILLIAM CLOWES AND SONS, LIMITED,
STAMFORD STREET AND CHARING CROSS.

PREFACE.

THE present publication is confined to a particular series of vases (kylikes), which, from the fact of their having designs both on the interior and exterior, could not be satisfactorily exhibited in the cases of the Museum without in a manner sacrificing one side or the other. Fortunately, it was found that the interiors lent themselves well to photography, and that with a photographic reproduction of each interior, exact both in line and colour, placed beside each vase, the exteriors could be displayed in a manner worthy of their greater importance as artistic compositions. To obtain adequate reproductions, it was necessary to transfer the photographs to process-blocks, and to print from them on a paper prepared with a terra-cotta colour resembling that of the vases.

This having been done, it was decided to utilize these blocks for a wider purpose, and to accompany them with a brief sketch of what is known of the artists who are represented in this particular series, and an outline of the more important questions that arise in connection with these vases. Such is the origin of the present publication.

The exteriors of these vases defy photography, but, where necessary in illustration of the special qualities of an artist, they have been introduced into the text from engravings which are known to have been made with the greatest care.

Opposite each plate is printed a brief description of each vase. These descriptions have been drawn up by Mr. CECIL SMITH, Assistant in the Department.

A. S. MURRAY.

1894.

DATE AND ARTISTIC QUALITIES OF THE VASES.

Among ancient nations the Greeks alone cultivated the art of pottery with brilliant success. Neither in Egypt nor in Assyria do we find painted vases which have any claim to be works of fine art. In Persia it was a mark of royal disfavour to be made to drink from earthenware.

Among the Greeks, no doubt, there were rich men who had a passion for vases of silver or of gold. The inventories of the treasures stored on the Acropolis of Athens—fragmentary as they are —tell us of the extent to which wealthy Athenians made gifts of silver vessels to the goddess Athenè. Still the truth remains that the number of Greek painted vases now to be seen in the museums of Europe is almost past reckoning, and that among them the element of artistic beauty, alike in quality and quantity, defies estimate.

But while the Greeks throughout their history were skilled in this art, it is remarkable that the period in which the general level of their workmanship reached its highest point was the period immediately preceding the full maturity of the art. What they were capable of achieving in the brief age when their powers were at their best may be seen on some of the Athenian vases which have drawings in outline on a white ground, as also on not a few of the red figured vases. Yet it is a fact that these splendid specimens of a perfected art stand out as exceptions among a large number of contemporary vases where carelessness is far too often a provoking element.

Again, while Greek sculpture and painting, after having passed their zenith, made some memorable efforts to hold their ground by means of new conceptions, new observation of nature and new technical skill, the vase painters when placed in similar circumstances attained no corresponding success. Their efforts, as in the introduction of polychrome designs on a certain class of vases, show that they quite appreciated what was required of them in the new direction of bright colouring. But they reveal also an incapacity to invent the new technical processes that were necessary for the occasion. Unfortunately the production of vases still went on with great activity on the simple lines of making them as bright as possible with such elementary technical processes as were at hand. Skill in drawing and composition very soon went overboard. Yet it is precisely this skill of

drawing and composition that casts so poetic a charm over the older vases, and never more potently than in the period which immediately preceded the full maturity of the art, when as yet the new sense of the beauty of colour was only beginning to exercise a powerful influence.

For some years it has been this preparatory stage, as it may be called, which has most attracted the students of Greek vase painting, and it is it that the vases here published illustrate as far as they go. It was a time of strenuous and prolific endeavour to prepare the way for a grand culmination of the art, which was indeed reached, but which was not proportionately sustained. That is one source of interest.

In many instances the vases of this period are signed with the names of the painters, and thus arouse the critical faculty to the task of observing the peculiarities of individual artists, comparing them and forming conclusions. The books that have resulted from this are a proof of the fascination of the subject. But this branch of the subject is not limited to actual signatures of vase painters. These artists frequently combined with their signatures the name of some person, to which they added the word "beautiful" (καλός), or some form of salutation; and from observing the regularity with which the artists used one or two such names, it has been argued that where these same names or forms of salutation occur alone they equally designate the painter of the vase, though he has not chosen to add his name. The evidence on this point is fairly conclusive. But it must be remembered that there are still a considerable number of the favourite or kalos names which have not yet been apportioned to particular vase painters, while, on the other hand, any day may bring to light proof that one or other of these artists had employed a greater variety of these names than is at present supposed. Till that happens, the only course is to judge these unappropriated kalos vases strictly by their style, and to class them as nearly as possible according to the schools of the known vase painters. That, again, is a fruitful occupation among students.

Of late years it has been remarked that among these popular or favourite names a limited number were borne by persons who were conspicuous in a particular period of Greek history, such as Hipparchos, Miltiades, Leagros, and Glaucon; and from this circumstance it has been argued that the vases in question had been painted contemporaneously with these celebrated men. They thus carry us back to the most momentous period of Greek history, a period which was signalised first by the expulsion from Athens of the Peisistratids in B.C. 510, which paved the way for freedom from the rule of tyrants at home, and secondly by the defeat of the Persians at Marathon (B.C. 490) and Salamis (B.C. 480), which secured freedom from foreign invasion. Thus in a political sense also that was a preparatory period for the Athenians, followed by a rapid maturity of all the great gifts of that people.

In B.C. 480 the Persians devastated the Acropolis of Athens, leaving behind them a stratum of ruin, which has been carefully explored in recent years. It is attested that many fragments of vases of the kind here published were found in that stratum, and so far the view is confirmed that the vase painters were contemporary with the famous men whose names they occasionally inscribed on the vases. At the same time, it must be owned that there is often a danger in excavating that objects properly belonging to one stratum may have in some unaccountable way got into another. Instances of that are known, and in the case of the Acropolis excavations there has been a certain amount of contention as to where particular fragments of pottery were actually found (Klein, 'Vasen mit Lieblingsinschriften,' p. 14).

The personality of the vase painters being a matter of deep interest to students, it is proposed to give here a brief account of those of them who are represented in the series of Plates now issued, and to note such peculiarities of style as may be gathered from a general review of their known works. These are Panphæos, Thypheithides, Epictetos, Chachrylion, Euphronios, Duris, Hieron, Brygos. Among the unsigned vases not a few are inscribed with names of favourites, as *Memnon kalos*, or *Chaerestratos kalos*, reminding us of the passage of Aristophanes, where Sitalkes of Thrace is described as being so fond of the Athenians that he wrote up on his walls, Ἀθηναῖοι καλοί, like those lovers who scrawl the name of the beloved on walls, or trees, or foliage (ἐν τοῖς τοίχοις ἢ δένδροις ἢ φύλλοις, see Scholiast ad Acharn. 144). It will be necessary to consider these names apart with a view of ascertaining, if possible, their position in the chronology of the vase painters. Many are entirely uninscribed, or at most have only the formula ὁ παῖς καλός. As regards these, the order in which they have been placed will be discussed by reference to peculiarities of style. In the present series there is only one example of the name of a prominent historical personage, viz., Hipparchos, on No. 22 (E 8). Nevertheless, as the question of the particular age to which the vases of this series belong largely turns on this point, it will be useful to follow up the matter in its principal aspects.

Meantime, as regards the series of designs reproduced in our Plates, it should be stated that they occur on the interiors of vases of the shape which the Greeks called a kylix—a large shallow circular dish with two handles and a high foot. The design in the interior is like a central medallion surrounded by a large space of black colour or varnish. In each instance in the present series the kylix has also a design on the exterior; but as these external designs are disposed over a surface which curves strongly in two directions—both horizontally and vertically—they cannot be reproduced by photography without distortion. For that reason they could not be included in the present series, where the object has been absolutely faithful reproduction, and where the attainment of this object has been rendered possible by the flat surface of the interiors on which these designs were painted. The only way in which these exterior drawings can be reproduced is by the process of tracing the individual figures carefully, then placing them on a flat surface of paper as nearly in their original composition as they will go. In the most important of the vases here under consideration this has been done as well as it is ever likely to be. In several instances we reproduce the results thus obtained, and insert them as text-illustrations (Figs. 1–9) when describing the characteristics of the several painters. There will be found also in the short descriptions which accompany our Plates references to the works in which these tracings have been published. It is highly advisable that the student should make free use of these publications because of the number of kindred vases which they contain from other Museums, and because the collection of the British Museum, though it is very rich in this respect, is not alone sufficient to illustrate all the peculiarities of style even of those vase painters from whose hands it possesses undoubted works. Moreover, it is evident that the curving surfaces of the exterior of a kylix must by the very difficulty of the task have challenged the best powers of the artists. The plain medallion-like group in the interior was in comparison a simple and genial piece of work. It attracted painters to whom grace of execution was more natural than fire of composition.

The vases here published are classed in the Museum under the letter E, and are usually quoted in archæological works as E 1, E 10, &c. These numbers are here retained, but for convenience of reference we have added running numbers to the Plates, and shall quote them in the following pages along with the E numbers.

As regards the chronological order of these vases, we have to distinguish two stages. The earlier stage, Nos. 1 to 26—we speak solely of interiors—is marked by great simplicity of design, one figure having been as a rule enough for the artist, while as regards the border round his design he was content with a plain circle. In the later stage, from No. 27 onwards, this border is rich and effective, the design expands into groups of two figures, freedom of action and freedom of drawing go on increasing, rich and varied details of drapery present no difficulties; they are rather sought after. But this change towards richness, freedom and excellence, though it is sufficiently striking, need not imply any great interval of time. It may very well have been accomplished during the career of some one prominent painter. The varying quality of the work of several of the painters suggests this view. In the meantime it is due to the earlier class—the pioneers so to speak of the red figured style of vase painting—to state that the simplicity of design which pervades their work is not always an enforced simplicity, but is at times a matter of choice. In the first specimens it was no doubt enforced, because at that time the painters were just emerging from the older method of black figures on red ground into the new and altogether different method of red figures on black ground. Some of the painters were still working in both processes. In other cases we see two painters at work on one vase, the one employing the new, the other the old process. What had been a special charm of the black figured vases—the free use of accessory colours, such as purples and whites, and the indications of patterns on costume by means of lines incised on the black—had to yield to pure outline drawing. It was a change from painting—of a kind which had numerous limitations imposed on it by the nature of its materials—to drawing, of a kind which had practically no limits imposed on it of a material nature. A change which involved such splendid possibilities would necessarily work slowly.[*]

Apparently it began with what we have called an enforced simplicity of design, which contented itself with a single figure within a circular space marked off by a thin red line. An instinct derived from older art dictated to the painters that this circular space must be broken up and taken full possession of by the figure within it. The figure must assume an attitude of stooping, kneeling, or running, such as would adapt it to this purpose. As W. Klein says (Euphronios, 2nd ed., p. 96), "Here we have carrying, lifting, hurrying, running, stooping, dancing, springing . . . . and all for the sole purpose of obtaining those movements of the human body which the space of the vase demanded." That was almost invariable. It was forced on the painters by tradition on the one hand, and by their still immature faculties on the other; in the earliest specimens the flexibility of the figures

is much more apparent than real. Gradually we see less and less of this limitation. Skill of drawing advances; yet for a time we see no signs of a desire to break away from the simplicity of design with which the new phase had begun. On the contrary, we recognise a studied endeavour to maintain that character of simplicity. This is conspicuous in the vases of Epictetos and of others who, though now nameless, worked in his manner and may have been in a general sense of his school.

It is no exceptional thing to find a studied or "affected" manner in the history of Greek vase painting. Among the latest black figure painters, Amasis and Exekias were conspicuous for it, so much so that a number of years ago one of the most competent judges in these matters announced his conviction that these painters had lived in a comparatively late age, and that their work was to be regarded as an attempt to revive a method of vase painting which had been for several centuries superseded. But whether it is in the nature of things that every new phase of art must run its course and end in affectation and mannerism, or whether external circumstances determine this, at one time in one way, at another time in another way, it is plain that the earlier class of red figured kylikes, while uniform in their aspect of simplicity of design, became studiously or even affectedly so as they went on. What we have specially to bear in mind is that the short period of Greek history within which the whole of the vases now in question fall was a period of extraordinary activity in every direction of intellect and genius, and that among the vast number of vase painters then at work in Athens, many would be old men grown up in traditions which they could not very readily shake off, while others would be young men eager to advance in their art. Yet there was no violent bursting of the old bonds. So far as we can see, the only excess was in the direction of adhering to tradition, with the effect of producing for a time a phase of affectation, which in the circumstances was probably not without its advantages.

To appreciate fully the advance in artistic quality which we have here indicated in a general way, it would be necessary to have before us an equally ample representation of the contemporary arts. As regards the higher walk of mural painting, which may be supposed to have been the chief inspiration for these vases, it is to be feared that the many famous works of this nature of which we read in ancient writers have entirely perished. On the other hand, there is in contemporary sculpture much that may be made available. The pediment sculptures of Ægina, now in Munich, irresistibly recall the scenes of combat on the exteriors of our kylikes, where we find a composition having a strongly marked centre, towards which the action hurries from each side, the figures linked together as if the conception had flowed from the artist's imagination in an unbroken stream, without intervals of grouping. Equally the kneeling, stooping, or advancing attitudes of the

---

[*] It has been supposed that this striking change had been brought about under the influence of Cimon of Cleonæ, whom Pliny in his often-quoted passage (N. Hist. xxxv, 56) describes as the first of the Greek painters to introduce what he calls *catagrapha*, which he proceeds to explain as "obliquas imagines et varie formare vultus respicientis suspicientisve vel despicientis; articulis membra distinxit, venas protulit praeterque in veste rugas et sinus invenit." And certainly these words indicate admirably the change in vase painting when the outline drawing of the red figured style succeeded the black silhouettes of the older period. See W. Klein, Euphronios, 2nd ed., p. 46.

combatants of Ægina adapt themselves to the circumscribed space of the pediment much as the figures in the interiors of many of the kylikes. It is, however, to the coins and engraved gems that we must look for the best analogies, and happily there is an abundance of contemporary coins and gems. It is true that the vase painter had a larger field to work on, a freer scope for his imagination in the composition of extensive groups of figures, and less necessity for minute exactness in details. But these advantages stood him in little stead when his task was confined to the circular space in the interior of a kylix, which, from its shape, we instinctively call a medallion, and thus suggest a comparison with the coins. It will be sufficient to indicate only a few specimens, taking them from the silver coinage of the Greeks which numismatists assign to *circa* B.C. 480-400, and choosing the earliest examples.

(1) Coin of Naxos : Satyr seated to front on ground. Compare the similarly seated figure on our Euphronios vase, No. 27 (F. 28), or, better, the Satyr seated to front on a wine-skin, which Klein (Euphronios, 2nd ed., p. 279) assigns to Euphronios.

(2) Coin of Chios : Sphinx. Compare No. 7 (E 19).

(3) Coin of Aspendus : armed warrior advancing. Compare No. 8 (E 9).

(4) Coin of Cos : disc thrower. Compare the youthful athlete, No. 55 (E 46).

Possibly somewhat earlier in date are—

(5) Coin of Poseidonia : Poseidon hurling trident. Compare No. 30 (E 48).

(6) Coin of Cnossos in Crete : the Minotaur. Compare No. 29 (E 49), or outside of No. 22 (E 8).

(7) Coin of Thebes : nude male figure kneeling on one knee and fitting string to bow. Compare No. 19 (E 52) with warrior kneeling and examining his arrow before fixing it to his bow.

Though the gems of this period were seldom precisely of this circular shape, yet the artistic faculty demanded of the engraver was the same, with this difference in his favour, that he was less hampered than the die-sinker by prescribed subjects. Apparently he was as free as the vase-painter in his choice of subject. He appealed to the same tastes and possibly often to the same patrons. The wealthy Etruscans, by whom nearly every one of the vases of this class in the Museum had been imported and ultimately consigned to the family tomb in Vulci, Cornetto, or elsewhere, imported also in considerable numbers engraved Greek gems. It would have been interesting, had regular statistics been kept of the finding of vases and gems, to see how far the coincidence of style which would be expected between the gems and the vases found in one tomb was confirmed. In some instances this has been noted, with a satisfactory result.

In Greece itself, and particularly in the island of Cyprus, a considerable number of gems have been found of late years carrying engravings which often recall the interiors of our kylikes. Among those found by General Cesnola, and engraved in pl. 39 of his work (Cyprus, &c.), Nos. 6, 7, 8 illustrate our point. They represent in each case a nude youthful male figure in the attitude of stooping, bending or kneeling. On another gem (Annali dell' Instituto, 1883, p. 213) we see two genii carrying off the body of Memnon or Sarpedon, and are at once reminded of the same subject on our vase signed by Panphaeos (Fig. 1), though doubtless the vase painter has in this instance at least excelled the gem engraver. Indeed he has so far surpassed himself that it has been questioned whether this particular side of the vase was actually by him, or might not have been by some greater artist like Euphronios (Klein, Euphronios, 2nd ed., p. 274), and whether his signature may not only refer to other parts, such as the interior, which is unmistakably his work. But an equally effective comparison may be made from the gems in the Museum collection, as for example :—No. 468, Heracles kneeling ; No. 470, Gorgon ; No. 472, Protesilaus and Laodameia ; No. 473, Capaneus ; No. 475, Apollo kneeling and playing on lyre ; No. 476, Sphinx. Among recent acquisitions from Greece, not included in the printed Catalogue of Gems, may be mentioned the representation of (1) a Satyr carrying a wine-skin on his back, (2) a youth holding in a horse (two specimens), (3) a youth stooping to fasten his sandal, (4) a figure of a bowman drawing his bow, with a dog at his feet, on a pale plasma and in the form of a scaraboid, as all the gems just mentioned are.

These, and other similar coincidences which could be cited on a wider review of the subject, show that the vase painters were in full sympathy with the spirit of their times. Doubtless they imposed on themselves a narrow choice of figures for their interiors. They might have found, as on the coins and gems, figures of deities, of heroes, or of animals, which could equally have been made to suit the circular space. Yet the fact remains that for this part of the vase they avoided, as a rule, any specialization of the figure beyond what its action obviously conveyed. Among the exceptions are No. 10 (E 18), with Eros, and No. 37 (E 62), with Hermes. Their chief task was on the exterior scenes, where they were far from averse to myth and legend with more or less of violence and action. To turn from such a scene of agitation or violence, and to find in the interior of the vase a single human figure represented in some simple attitude, instantly intelligible and complete within itself- -as in No. 21 (E 13), with the labours of Theseus outside and a simple youthful figure inside—is to enjoy a sense of repose. We do not say that this is always the case. In one kylix in the Museum (E 53) we see the labours of Theseus both on the exterior and interior, the single groups of figures being ingeniously placed through from each other, if we may so describe it. At each point of the vase we have the same group, inside and outside. The vase is finely drawn, but the effect is of a worrying description, and did not apparently find favour. An exception of a very different kind is when the painter employs the interior of the vase for a special scene in the dramatic development of the groups on the exterior, as in the case of two very good kylikes by Euphronios. The one is in Perugia (Klein, Euphronios, 2nd ed., pp. 214, 215, 220), and represents the legend of Troilos. On the outside we see first a scene of preparation for battle; next, Achilles seizing the youth Troilos by the hair, the horses escaping wildly; and in the interior Achilles slaying Troilos at an altar. The other kylix is in the Louvre (Klein, Euphronios, 2nd ed., p. 182), and bears on the outside a series of the labours of Theseus, while in the interior is what may be described as his crowning deed—when Minos had cast his ring into the sea, and challenged Theseus to go and bring it up. Here we observe Theseus rising from the sea, borne upwards on the hands of a Triton, in the presence of the sea-goddess Amphitrite and of Athenè. The same subject was known in antiquity from a mural painting by Micon in the Theseum at Athens, but in an abridged form, and already injured by time in the 2nd cent. A.D. (Pausanias, I. 17, 3).

While in many instances the figure or group in the interior has no apparent connection with the scenes on the outside, there is on the other hand a large number of vases where the interior is either a sort of epitome of the exterior, or a continuation of the same. Of the former class are—No. 40 (E 23, ext., musical scenes : int., a musical group of two figures); No. 48 (E 27, ext., banquet scenes : int., one such group); No. 31 (E 39, ext., groups of young men and young women : int., one young woman); No. 35 (E 42, Satyrs and Maenads : int., one Maenad); No. 30 (E 48, ext., banquet scenes : int., a single figure holding a drinking cup); No. 19 (E 52, ext., battle scenes : int., an archer fitting his bow); No. 49 (E 63, ext., banquet with music of flutes : int., one flute player). As examples of interiors which seem to indicate a continuation or development of the exterior, we may note—No. 34 (E 40, ext., figures going to banquet: int., two figures in same act); No. 24 (E 44, ext., athletes exercising : int., athlete at altar) ; No. 55 (E 46, ext., again athletes exercising : int., a young athlete standing before a paidotribes); No. 46 (E 47, ext., banquet scenes : int., girl dancing before a single banqueter). Slightly different are the two vases of Epictetos, No. 23 (E 7) and No. 22 (E 8), where the interiors answer to only one side of the exteriors.

It may be said with truth that these examples have been drawn from a comparatively limited series of vases. But it is equally true that the question before us is a limited one, viz : whether and how far the interior designs respond to the exteriors. In any case it is a question which the student of vases should bear in mind, just because of the opportunity it affords of tracing the working of the mind and imagination of the painters.

The experience of the past few years has tended to modify the date to which vases of the class here published were previously assigned. It had been almost an article of faith that the beginning of the red figure painting could not be put earlier than B.C. 480, when the Persians destroyed the Acropolis of Athens. No one listened when Ludwig Ross claimed that the fragment of a vase of this kind, which he found in his excavations on the south side of the Parthenon, belonged to the stratum of ruin which the Persians had then left behind. This claim, as we have already said, has now been confirmed (Jahrbuch, 1893 : Arch. Anz. p. 13) by an elaborate investigation of the fragments discovered on the same site in recent years. Even previous to this investigation the result had been accepted in general terms by the most critical of all writers on Greek vases, W. Klein (Vasen mit Lieblingsinschriften, 1890, p. 14).

It does not follow, however, that because some of these vases are older than B.C. 480, they are necessarily much older. That is where the difficulty comes in. Take for instance this result : a recent excavation into the tumulus at Marathon has brought to light one red figure fragment among a number of black figure vases, thus showing that the red figure method was in use in B.C. 490, but shewing also that the prevalent method was then that of the black figures (Ath. Mittheilungen, xviii., p. 56). Meanwhile one party would push the red figures back to the age of the Peisistratids, whose tyranny in Athens ended B.C. 510. Klein and others would assign to a short period immediately preceding B.C. 480 only the earlier stage of this class of vases —those associated with the names of Panphaeos and Epictetos. In this they are influenced largely by such coincidences between the vases and the higher art of mural painting as we have just noticed in the case of the vase of Euphronios with the Theseus incident in its relation to the painting by Micon. There is no possibility of doubt that the painting of Micon was executed after B.C. 480. It is even thought that Euphronius may have seen the picture in the course of execution. Nor is this a solitary instance. The style of the great mural painter, Polygnotos, so far as it can be discovered from ancient writers, appears to be reflected on the vases of the Euphronios epoch.

The latest writer on this subject, P. Hartwig, who has just published a magnificent work on the Meisterschalen, says (p. 154) that the date now ascertained for Euphronios from the Acropolis excavations has brushed aside for ever the old notions of a relation between the work of that artist and that of the great mural painter Polygnotos. It may be so, but there is another argument which has also to be considered. The age of Polygnotos was the age when Kimon ruled the political life of Athens. It was Kimon who brought back the bones of Theseus from Skyros to Athens, and it was under his influence that a new cultus of Theseus arose in Athens. It has been observed that at a particular stage in their development the vase painters made, so to speak, a rush for the legend of Theseus, treating him as a sort of a second Heracles, and it is argued that this had been due to the new movement under Kimon. That may be fairly allowed. But it has been argued further that these Theseus, and therefore Kimonian, vases take us back to close on the beginning of the red-figure style. That is open to question. The freedom both in composition and drawing which signalises the Theseus vases, as compared with those of the older stage, may well have taken a considerable time to acquire.

It seems, however, impossible to determine the length of time occupied in that earlier stage, unless we accept the other view, that a certain number of the names of favourite persons inscribed on the vases in question were the names of contemporaries who in their day had been conspicuous in Athens. But this view has also its difficulties. It is understood that the large number of favourite names on the vases indicate youths. Therefore those historic names of Hipparchos, Miltiades, Leagros and others could not have been inscribed on the vases in consequence of the fame of these men, who must still have been mere youths when the vases were painted. The names of sons of prominent citizens would naturally appear on the vases, whether these youths afterwards became distinguished or not. As it happens, the majority by far are lost in oblivion. Yet probable and reasonable as this explanation may seem in its general bearings, there is clearly some room for hesitation before finally accepting a theory in which chance is so considerable an element; the more so in our imperfect knowledge of Greek usage in the matter of proper names. We cannot be sure that the notorious Hipparchos, who was slain in the streets of Athens B.C. 514, is the man whose name appears on a number of vases. He may have been and probably was very popular a number of years before, when still a young man and a scion of the ruling family. But there was another Hipparchos, who was archon at Athens in B.C. 496. He equally in his youth may have fascinated the vase-painters. It has been argued also (Hellenic Journal, xii., p. 380) that if we take the name of Hipparchos, not as that of the tyrant, but as that of his brother-in-law, who remained in Athens down to B.C. 488, we obtain a more satisfactory chronology for our vases.

As regards Miltiades, we can readily believe that in his youth he was an attractive person in Athens. But the occurrence of his name in conjunction with the figure of a mounted Persian on a vase at Oxford would indicate him as the conqueror of Marathon, and not as a boy. Either, then, we must give up the theory that these names always refer to youths, or assume a later Miltiades, who as a youth may in this manner have been popularized by a vase painter. The name of Charmides on a vase may remind us that Plato has immortalized this name, or it may recall the father of Pheidias, or again it may refer to some unknown youth in an intermediate period. On a red figure hydria in this Museum

(E 264) by the painter Phintias, we read the famous name of Megacles, possibly the Megacles who was ostracised B.C. 487. To complicate matters, we have a number of vases bearing the name, in a favourite sense, of the legendary hero Memnon, who was famed for his beauty in Homer. It is highly improbable that any family in Athens would have adopted this name for one of its sons. There would have been no objection to it as the name of a slave, or in the lower grades of society. Certain of the grosser comic poets mention a Memnon, whom they associated with Panaitios and Hippocrates, calling the sons of all three "pigs" (Meineke, ii. p. 23). And apparently the Panaitios here referred to was the man whom Aristophanes described as an "ape," the scholiast adding that he was the son of a cook (Meineke, ii. p. 1111). Panaitios was certainly a name of some distinction in Athens, and the vase painters, contrary to the habits of the comic poets, may have always chosen persons of exalted position; in which case the name of Panaitios, as used by the vase painters, might indicate the associate of Alkibiades in the mutilation of the Hermae at Athens. In short, we have still to fathom the principle on which the vase painters chose their favourite names, if these names are to be of true service in determining dates.

Meantime the urgent question is that of artistic style. If, in respect of style, we can satisfy ourselves that the vases bearing the names of Leagros and Glaucon belong to the first half of the 5th cent. B.C., then we may fairly associate them with the Leagros who commanded and fell in battle B.C. 467, and who twenty years or so before may have been a beautiful youth in Athens (say B.C. 487), and with his son Glaucon, who was in command in Corcyra B.C. 432, and whose youth in Athens may have been at its brightest B.C. 455; thus far there is little or no difficulty. We may accept with Klein the period of B.C. 490-455 as that of the Leagros and Glaucon vases, and therefore the period of the greatest of the vase painters, Euphronios. But we have also to satisfy ourselves that the artistic style of the vases which bear the name of Hipparchos represents an interval of time reaching back to at least B.C. 525, at which date we may place his youth, he having been slain, as we have said, B.C. 514. Unquestionably there was an interval of time between the two sets of vases. It is enough to compare the vase with the name Hipparchos engraved by Klein (Vasen mit Lieblingsinschriften, p. 30), with the identical subject on a vase having a different name (Panaitios) in Klein's Euphronios, 2nd ed., p. 278, to recognise at once the greater artistic freedom of the latter. Yet it is just such a change as one artist might easily have experienced within a year or two in his own life; and when Klein, identifying this Hipparchos vase with the painter Epictetos, assigns it to the age of Themistocles, instead of to the older age of the Athenian tyrants, he appears to allow a fairly sufficient interval for the progress that was made between then and the period of Leagros and

Glaucon. On this view the two vases by Epictetos in the present series, Nos. 23 and 22 (E 7, E 8), the latter of which bears the name "Hipparchos," will fall in the momentous epoch between the battles of Marathon (B.C. 490) and Salamis (B.C. 480); while No. 27 (E 28), one of the late works of Euphronios, may be assigned to about B.C. 460.

We proceed now to notice some of the peculiarities of the vase painters, beginning with

PANPHAIOS.—This painter may be said to have stood with one foot in the black figure and the other in the red figure period. At a time of transition the like of this may not have been uncommon. But while others may have changed lightly enough from the old order to the new, it is to the credit of Panphaios that he did his best to excel in the black figure method before abandoning it. We see this in our hydria by him (B 300), where in his endeavours to make the black figures attractive he has indulged to excess his sense of

of Memnon. Surely in the whole realm of Greek vase painting there is hardly to be met with a finer conception. No wonder that it has been ascribed to the greatest of vase painters, Euphronios. There is a largeness and breadth of style—especially in the figure of Memnon—which instantly suggest that name. And yet the vase bears on its foot the signature of Panphaios, while the interior design—a figure of Silenus—is unmistakably an example of his ordinary work. More than that, we recognise on the exterior a distinct reminiscence of the older method of Panphaios in the border of black palmettes. There is only one reason for thinking him incapable of the Memnon scene, and that is its great beauty. But let us see. In the Museum stamnos (E 438), bearing a group of Heracles wrestling with Acheloös, we have an opportunity of comparing his artistic powers with those of another painter, Timagoras, who had chosen the same subject for a hydria now in the Louvre (Vorlegeblätter, 1889, pl. 5, fig. 3c). While the

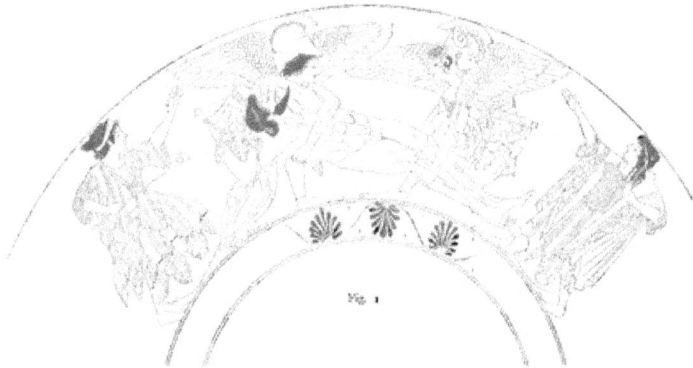

Fig. 1

refinement and grace. In those qualities he was not alone, but he was unsurpassed. When, however, he turned to red figures, his former minuteness of finish appears to have failed him. He could not employ it except by means of new technical processes which were only beginning to be understood. That may explain in a measure how his red figure kylikes came to be as a rule comparatively coarse in execution, as on the exterior of No. 8 (E 9) and the interior of No. 9 (E 10). But there is more than that to take into consideration. There is a freshness and vigour of conception which seem to imply that when he made the change from the one method to the other, he did it as one who had exhausted the old method and now perceived that what was necessary was a strong robust art. But even keeping this in mind, we must be prepared for a surprise when we turn to Fig. 1 (one of the exterior scenes on No. 9 = E 10), where two wind gods carry off the body

latter is stiff, cramped and truly archaic, Panphaios, without altering the general conception, or losing its force, has imported into it a new sense of beauty and grace which is so full of promise that one is inclined to hesitate before denying absolutely that the Memnon scene was within the reach of that painter. One of the most noticeable of the details in the Memnon scene is the long joints of the fingers and toes, bent and suggestive as they are of a firm, tenacious grip. Undoubtedly Euphronios knew well how to draw such hands; but though the hands of Memnon and of one of the genii are surely as beautiful as even he could have rendered them, still there were other vase painters who could draw the hand with admirable suggestiveness of a firm grip, and among them was Panphaios. He knew that the great beauty of feet and hands resided in the long rigid joints, and in respect of them there is perhaps nothing in the Memnon scene which he could not have executed.

It is a different question when we come to the largeness and breadth of style in the Memnon scene, which, as we have said, immediately suggest Euphronios, as does also the rendering of the inner markings of muscles and bones by faint yellow lines. See for example our kylix Fig. 4 (No. 27 = E 28), which may be taken as a fair example of the manner of Euphronios. So far one would readily accept the Memnon scene as by him. What it lacks is the excessive concentration which he throws into his work. Take as an instance of this concentration the vase just mentioned (Fig. 4), and compare with it a vase in the Louvre having exactly the same subjects (Vorlegeblätter, 1890-91, pl. 10): on one side the legend of Heracles and Eurystheus, on the other side a chariot group. A moment's examination will show how Euphronios has modified the older conception, as seen in the Louvre vase, in the direction of concentrated action and power, to say nothing of the new wealth of details which he has introduced in costume and

the full extent of his versatility may as yet be unknown, and that he actually signed our Memnon vase, we are bound in his interest to suspend judgment.

THYPHEITHIDES is known in our collection by only one vase, No 1 (E 4), where he paints the interior figure black and the exterior red, in neither instance with any excellence. He appears to be an example of the ordinary run of artists of the transition stage from black to red figures.

HISCHYLOS and PHEIDIPPOS.—No. 3 (E 5) bears the name of Hischylos as the maker of the vase (ἐποίησεν), the exterior being signed by the painter Pheidippos, who otherwise is not at present known. On another of our kylikes (E 3, not here published), Hischylos again appears as the "maker," but this time in conjunction with the celebrated painter, Epictetos, who signs with ἔγραφσεν. In general, Hischylos is held to have been a potter rather than a painter.

EPICTETOS.—No painter is so uniform and at the

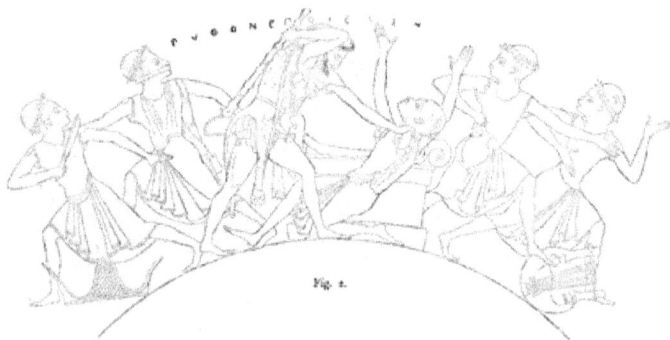

Fig. 2.

otherwise. In our Memnon scene we do not find anything like this extent of concentration, and, on the other hand, we do find that its largeness of style is accompanied by a greater refinement of lines, both in the inner markings and the contours, than was usual with Euphronios, whose lines on Fig. 4, and generally, are thick and of a different character. No doubt if we assume that Euphronios painted the Memnon scene, that would involve accepting him as a contemporary of Panphaeos, but necessarily a younger man, who was as yet painstaking in detail and not mature in his powers of concentration. We know that a vase painter did not always expressly sign his work. He contented himself often with the name of a favourite, and for all we know to the contrary, he may at times have allowed his vases to go forth without any recognisable sign beyond what he conceived would be apparent in the workmanship. The question is a difficult one; and bearing in mind that Panphaeos was a versatile artist, that

same time so peculiar in his manner as Epictetos. His drawing is always characterised by precision and fastidiousness. He loves slim youthful forms, where his qualities of drawing have perfect scope. He prefers to draw his figures on a small scale, where his minute touches produce at times a startling vividness. He appears to have been influenced in a measure by the older miniature vase painters of the black figure age, ordinarily known as the minor vase painters (in Germany, Kleinmeister). He likes a flat surface to work on, because there every line tells at one and the same moment. But his manner is singularly precise and fastidious, even when he takes in hand the exterior of a kylix and extends his choice of figures to old men, to horses, or to legendary subjects, such as Fig. 2, one of the scenes on the exterior of No. 23 (E 7), where Heracles slays Busiris to the consternation of his Egyptian followers; or that on No. 22 (E 8), where Theseus slays the Minotaur. In both scenes vigorous action had to be expressed, in both there is drapery to be dealt with as well as nude forms. But his precision never fails him; nor does it in a marked degree interfere with a due expression of the heroic element in these two scenes. The figure of the Minotaur is a very beautiful and bold conception, while the action of Heracles is strongly rendered. Epictetos uses skilfully faint yellow lines for the inner markings of muscle and bone.

Each of these two vases has also a banqueting scene on the exterior. In such subjects, the art of Epictetos found a more normal expression. We may note particularly the interior of No. 23 (E 7), with its group of a flute player and a dancer, as an example of the precision and fastidiousness of this painter. On the exterior (Fig. 2) a point of detail may be noticed, viz., that Heracles wears a short chiton under his lion's skin, as usual in the black figure period, whence the intimate relation of Epictetos to that period may be inferred. That, indeed, is put beyond doubt by our vase E 3, on which, as already said, we have in the interior a

CHACHRYLION.—The interiors of No. 26 (E 14) and No. 25 (E 15), which we reproduce from two vases signed by this artist, illustrate in some measure his individuality. Though still archaic in his manner, there is an obvious tendency in him towards being expressive and attractive without either violent action, such as Pamphæos was inclined to, or an exaggerated refinement in the types of his figures, such as Epictetos loved. He was in search of gracefulness, but without surrendering his natural robustness of temperament. On the exterior of No. 26 (E 14), where Theseus is carrying off Antiopeia, no one is in the least excited except Antiopeia (Fig. 3). There is hardly any movement. It seems clear that Chachrylion had lived in the earliest age of red figure painting, while as yet the older black figure method was being abundantly practised around him. He was keenly susceptible to the effect of minute details, which the black figure painters loved, while, on the other hand, his natural instincts were towards the

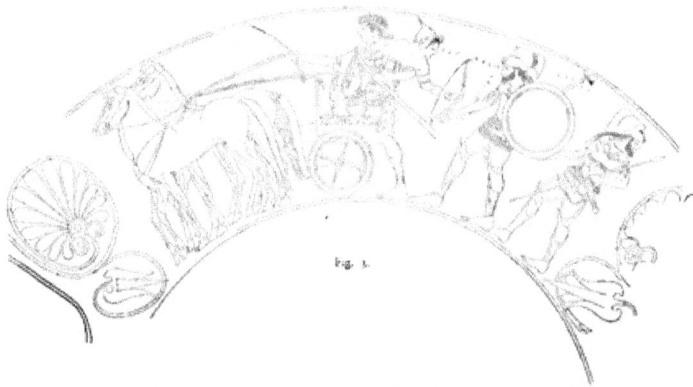

Fig. 3.

black design by Hischylos, and on the exterior in red a figure of Seilenos between two large symbolic eyes by Epictetos. Some go so far as to believe that this new method owed more to him than to any other painter. Be this as it may, he certainly exercised a powerful influence on his contemporaries, and he may even be said to have inspired the style of the later painter Duris, so far at least as concerns those banquet scenes which both artists delighted to paint. Epictetos appears to have always signed his vases with the word ἔγραφσεν, "painted," never with ἐποίησεν, "made," from which it has been inferred that he was strictly only a vase painter, not a potter as well. But such inferences are hardly safe in our present state of knowledge. No. 23 (Fig. 2) bears the name of Python as the maker (ἐποίησεν) along with that of Epictetos as the painter (ἔγραφσεν). On the interior of No. 22 (E 8) Epictetos employs the favourite name of "Hipparchos," for which see p. 6.

new and more virile manner, which Euphronios was soon to carry perhaps to excess. To say that the interiors of No. 26 (E 14) and No. 25 (E 15) are sufficient witnesses of this artistic element in Chachrylion might be saying too much. But an examination of the exteriors of these two vases, still better an examination of all the known works of this artist, will tend to confirm this statement. He is known to have worked along with Euphronios on a vase in Munich, which is signed by him with ἐποίησεν and by Euphronios with ἔγραφσεν, besides having also the favourite name "Leagros." That circumstance prepares us to expect, on occasion, some effort towards Euphronian largeness of style, such as we see in our kylix (E 104, not here published), with a youthful figure kneeling, inscribed with one of his favourite names, "Epidromos" (Hartwig, pl. 3, fig. 1). But, confining ourselves to the exteriors of our two kylikes signed by him, we cannot fail to observe that on

Fig. 3 there is combined with his excessive minuteness of detail a sturdiness, so to speak, in his figures which contrasts singularly with the work of Epictetos, who, in respect of minuteness and vividness of detail, so closely resembles him. Chachrylion treated his details of armour, dress, &c., always as details. However microscopic he might make them, they did not lead him to over-refine his types of figures. There is a vase of his with a youth sitting on a rock and fishing in the sea with a rod and net. The subject is by no means realistically rendered, and the conception may not have been originally his own, but the mere choice of a subject so singular for a vase implies on his part a certain love of natural life in the open air (Hartwig, pl. 5). Or, again, if we compare a fragmentary vase by him (Hartwig, pl. 4), representing Heracles slaying Busiris, with the same subject by Epictetos on the exterior of our kylix, Fig. 2, we see how he adheres to the general

word may very well include the latter, he may be supposed to have been both potter and painter. Of the class of vases bearing the name of " Memnon," to which we have just referred, the Museum possesses four specimens—No. 15 (E 31), No. 14 (E 32), No. 13 (E 34), No. 12 (E 35). A glance at these interiors will show that if they are by Chachrylion, he must at the time of painting them have been in an early stage of his career, before even the influence of Epictetos had taken a good hold of him. It has been thought that something of the style of Epictetos is traceable in No. 15 (E 31), with its kneeling warrior. Compared with the Amazon in No. 25 (E 15), which is signed by Chachrylion, this warrior is hard and wanting in tenderness of sentiment. On the other hand, No. 14 (E 32), with its female figure stooping to put on her sandal, though fine and even bold in conception, is still quite archaic in the type of face. We are not surprised that something of the manner

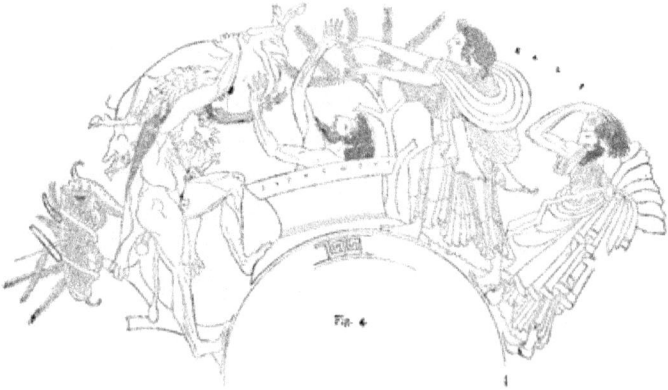

Fig. 4.

composition and the details of drapery of Epictetos, as if to the work of his master, while at the same time he infuses into the whole a fresh and vigorous spirit, suggestive of a new influence such as that of Euphronios—not Euphronios in his ripest and most mature stage, but in his earlier period, when he employed, in common with Chachrylion, the favourite names "Leagros" and "Epidromos." Later on, when Euphronios adopted the name "Panaitios," which is not found on any of the vases by Chachrylion, it is supposed that by that time Chachrylion must have passed over to the majority, or at all events ceased working.

His use of the favourite name "Memnon" concurs with the view that the earlier part of the life and work of Chachrylion had been spent in the period immediately preceding the advent of Euphronios. Chachrylion always signed his vases with the word ἐποίησεν, never with ἔγραφσεν; and as the former

of Panphæos has been recognised in this figure. The interiors of No. 13 (E 34) and No. 12 (E 35) belong to a very early stage of red figure painting. But on the exterior of the latter are a scene of Dionysos and Satyrs, which points either to Panphæos or Chachrylion (No. 25, E 15), and a scene of a chariot group, which recalls specially Chachrylion. So that, on the whole, we may fairly regard him as the possible painter of this vase, if not also of the others with the name of "Memnon."

EUPHRONIOS.—From the hand of this artist the Museum possesses only one signed vase, No. 27 (E 28); but see also Fig. 1, p. 7, ante. But it is a work of his ripest period and is constantly quoted in books on Greek vase painting. The interior bears the favourite name "Panaitios," which, as we have already had occasion to say, was used by him in his best and strongest work, his other favourite names being "Leagros," "Lycos," and "Glaucon." In this instance, the interior consists of a group of two figures—the one a man seated to the front and drawn with bold foreshortening, for which some employ the ancient term *catagrapha* or *obliquae imagines*; the other, a female figure standing by his side. The faces of both, with their large prominent noses, are eminently characteristic of Euphronios at this stage of his career, as is also his treatment of the drapery, where the fine folds of the woman's dress are no longer executed according to routine; by means of a slight perspective and freedom of drawing they assume a distinctness and reality which is refreshing to observe. In the exterior scenes of this vase Euphronios treats his draperies with perfect freedom, making them yield to any action he pleases, and constituting them more than ever an element of composition. One of these scenes is given in Fig. 4, where Heracles hurls down the boar on Eurystheus, who has taken refuge in a *pithos*.

But one of the most charming of his studies in this respect is the interior of the Theseus kylix in the Louvre, to which we have already referred.

Another vase in the Louvre, in the shape of a crater, shows us Euphronios when he was in the mood of drawing massive limbs and colossal proportions. The subject is the wrestling contest of Heracles and the giant Antaeos in the presence of three female figures, who are of course small in comparison with the two wrestlers. Both wrestlers are down on the ground, the attitude of Heracles reminding us of the scene so frequent on the black figure vases where he seizes the lion. In this position of the chief figures Euphronios was able to express forcibly the hugeness of the bodily forms without altogether dwarfing the female figures, and doubtless he had in this instance availed himself of the old black figure manner of wrestling on the ground instead of standing upright as in later art. This is the more probable because the

type of face in each case and the drapery of the female figures would naturally lead us to assign the Louvre vase to a comparatively early period in the life of the painter. To this period also, though not before he had manifestly acquired much of his subsequent largeness of style, belongs a kylix in our Museum (not here published, but see Hartwig, pl. 8), inscribed with the name "Leagros," a name which he employed in common with some contemporaries of his youth who up to a particular point worked in the same manner as himself—the manner of Epictetos. Again, something is to be said in support of our No. 28 (E 51) as a work of Euphronios. It is true that the group of two Amazons in the interior has none of his obvious characteristics, and is in fact very like an interior by Duris (Hartwig, pl. 22), but the figure of Heracles striking down an Amazon on the exterior has much of the manner of Euphronios (Fig. 5). The run-away horse on the other side has a strong resemblance to one of the horses

Fig. 5.

on the famous Troilos kylix (Hartwig, pl. 53). Our vase, Fig. 5, may therefore be classed as possibly his work. The Troilos vase is now in the Museum of Perugia, having up for a time disappeared (Klein, Euphronios, 2nd ed., p. 213). Its recovery has led to its being compared with a vase in the Louvre, which is signed by Euphronios as the maker and Onesimos as the painter. But in the Troilos vase the signature of Euphronios alone ought to be an indication sufficient for us that it is his work. There is, it is true, no trace on it of the almost rude power of expression which Euphronios employed on our No. 27 (E 28), and on several other vases, where the sense of this power within himself may be blamed for leading him to choose coarse, even disgusting subjects, such as that of drunken men vomiting. Yet there is no mistaking in it the presence of all the best and strongest qualities of Euphronios, though in a more subdued and more poetic form. His draperies in the interior of our vase No. 27 (E 28) are full of refinement and beauty. He had nothing to alter in that respect on the Troilos vase. Our No. 39 (E 45), with a boy on horseback, may be by Onesimos. It is a beautiful work and full of artistic individuality. The horse is drawn with such vigour and strength as a pupil of Euphronios may well have developed, while the contrasted smallness and refinement of the rider is more suggestive of the new influence of Duris.

Lastly, we must notice the work of Euphronios as a painter of vases having polychrome figures on a white ground. In the Berlin Museum there is a fragmentary kylix of this kind which bears his signature, together with the favourite name of "Glaucon." As regards "Glaucon," we have already stated the argument that this name, as employed here and elsewhere, was intended to celebrate a person well known to history, whose father, also a famous historical person, was named "Leagros," and that the difference of style between the vases of Euphronios which bear the name of "Leagros" and the one which bears the name of "Glaucon" represents a difference of time as between father and son. The Berlin vase must therefore fall in the later period of this artist's career. It certainly possesses breadth and largeness of style, but not enough of his known manner. Possibly in this case also he had a pupil or younger co-worker, who was better able to share in the new movements of art. We are unwilling as yet to accept the most recent view, viz., that Euphronios in this case only gives his name as the potter, and that the name of the actual painter has been lost, all but a few letters. The heads of the figures in the interior are of a more advanced type than we expect in his work. The lower part of the face has become massive and almost heavy, the chin presenting a strong and attractive outline, while the profile of the upper part of the face no longer slopes back, but is nearly vertical, the whole type of head recalling the largeness, simplicity, and nobility of the sculptures of Olympia. It is a type of head which is more or less characteristic of Duris, Hieron, and Brygos, to mention only artists directly represented in our collection who were, in a measure, contemporaries of Euphronios, though of a younger generation and sharing the progress of their time. It is a beautiful piece of work, and full of the individuality of the artist. But, if we reject the Berlin vase on this view, we can hardly accept as his work our polychrome kylikes, D 61 (Birth of Pandora) and D 62 (Aphrodite riding on swan), even though the latter is inscribed with the favourite name "Glaucon." On the other hand, our fragments of a polychrome kylix from Naucratis (Hartwig, pl. 50) may fairly be classed under his name. The head of the figure in the interior strongly recalls his manner.

Among the contemporaries of the early period of Euphronios was Euthymides, who, in one instance (on a vase in Munich), describes his own work as better than Euphronios had ever done (ὡς ὀυδέποτε

Εὐφρόνιος), a boast which, though far from justified by the vase, is interesting to us now as showing that the name of Euphronios was apparently a synonym in his day for the greatest excellence in vase painting.

Duris.—No less than 23 signed vases by this painter are known. To these may be added not a few others, which clearly proclaim themselves as proceeding from him, though he may not have considered them worthy of his signature. Thus it would seem, unless mere chance has preserved so many of his works in comparison with those of his contemporaries, that his peculiarly fine technical skill had been much appreciated in his day. Of that skill our two kylikes No. 30 (E 48) and No. 29 (E 49) are typical specimens. In the former we see his love of slim nude figures. In this instance, as in many others, the nude is contrasted with drapery, which is drawn with care and formality. Peculiar to him also are the shape of the head with its high cranium, the eye with its pupil marked by a circle with a dot in its centre. Like his predecessor, Epictetos, he was almost the slave of precision and of a desire to see everything in its right place. As a rule, he avoided violence of action, but rather sought after a quiet gracefulness, as in the vase now before us, No. 30 (E 48). So peculiarly his own is this characteristic of Duris, that wherever we find it on a vase we have no hesitation in assigning that vase to him, though it may not bear any name.

As instances we may quote Nos. 31-36. The designs on the exteriors of these vases consist of groups of inactive, complacent figures, except No. 34 (E 40) and No. 33 (E 41), where there is some action, and where in particular the painter has made free use of a new principle of composition, in which nude forms are set against a background of drapery with a fine decorative effect. Compare the interiors of No. 34 (E 40) and No. 38 (E 64). The severity and precision of the drawing in the nude forms are enhanced by the vagueness of the lines of drapery behind them; and though Duris may not have been the first to recognise this element of beauty—we find it in the work of Hieron and Brygos also—yet he uses it with a singular charm. It may even be said to be a natural development of his manner.

In No. 29 (E 49) a marked change has come over the manner of Duris, apparently from the influence of Euphronios. He no longer hesitates at violent action, as we see from the interior of this vase, where Theseus slays the Minotaur; and this group is matched by others on the exterior, in particular the noble group of Theseus and the robber Skiron (Fig. 6), which at once recalls the same subject on one of the kylikes of Euphronios (Vorlegeblätter, ser. v., pl. 1, fig. 2), and reminds us that the two artists used in common the favourite name "Panaitios." In his previous work, as on the exterior of No. 30 (E 48), Duris had shown a disposition towards very bold foreshortening, though confining it to figures in repose. His potentiality for violent action only required to be roused, and here for once at least that was done. But he still retains in the Theseus his own particular type of head and his own treatment of bodily forms, while obviously following Euphronios in his costumes and vigour of action—not the Euphronios of the pronounced manner of our Fig. 4, but in his more temperate work, as in the vase just quoted, and in the Troilos vase, if we are still to associate this vase with his name. It is only right, however, to mention that Hartwig (Meisterschalen, p. 614) finds much of the influence of Brygos, none of Euphronios, in the work of Duris. But whatever the influence, we still see in the interior of our Theseus vase how strong in Duris was the old sense of decorating a given space and making it attractive. The designs of Euphronios also may be said to decorate given spaces, but they eventually burst their bonds and introduce refinement in execution and in conception, in some respects recalling Duris, though having more vitality than he usually can command. This vase (No. 55) has been assigned to a painter at present only known from his use of the favourite name "Diogenes."

In one instance Duris signs his name with both ἔγραφσεν and ἐποίησεν. This is on a vase which bears the favourite name of his early period, "Chaerestratos," and has strong traces of Euphronios in the draperies. Lastly, we may mention E 784, which is signed by him, and a small kylix lately acquired by the Museum, bearing one of his favourite names of later times, "Hippodamas." These two vases, however, need not here be discussed. They contribute nothing new in point of style.

HIERON.—At present there are known twenty-eight vases signed by this artist. His custom is

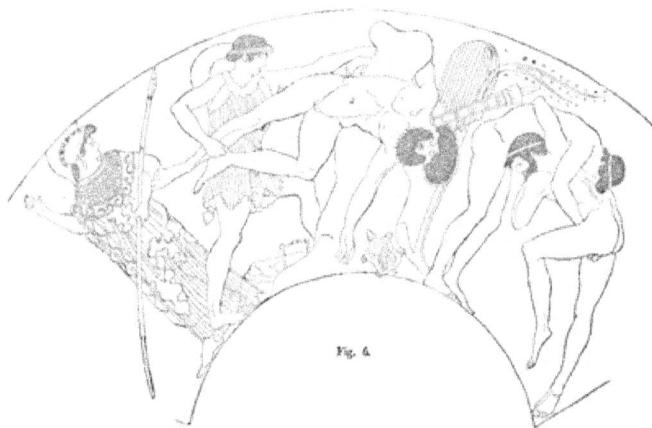

Fig. 4.

a striking vitality which almost defies the limits of the vase. That was what Duris did not attain to.

As an example of the earlier work of Duris we have No. 24 (E 44), which is signed by him on the exterior, and on the interior bears the favourite name "Chaerestratos," which he seems to have employed in his earlier days. On the exterior are groups of young athletes exercising in the palaestra. The huge torsos of the boxers present a curious contrast to the usually over-refined manner of Duris. Much the same is to be seen on the exterior of No. 55 (E 46), where two wrestlers go the length of trying to gouge out each other's eyes, and where in general it may be said that the roughness of the behaviour of the athletes is matched by roughness in their bodily forms and artistic rendering; whereas in the interior of the vase we have a group of considerable

to incise his name on the handle, adding always the word ἐποίησεν, which, where it occurs alone on a vase, as it frequently does, may be fairly held to indicate that the whole of the artistic work on the vase was by the person who signs it. Hieron was a contemporary of Duris, and was so far associated with him that both employ the favourite name "Hippodamas." But he was also definitely associated with another painter, Macron, who now is only known from one vase where he gives his name as the painter (ἔγραφεν) side by side with Hieron, who there employs his usual and more general term, ἐποίησεν. What is remarkable is that this vase, where Hieron has called in the aid of Macron, is of much finer and greater artistic quality than any of the numerous vases signed by Hieron alone. It is not, however, a difference of kind, but of degree; and this has led to the surmise that possibly all the other vases signed by Hieron were only his work as potter, while actually the painter of them all may have been this Macron. But that seems making twenty difficulties where at present there is only one. Certainly the vase in question is unrivalled for the dignity and grace of the figures.

Our Museum possesses two vases signed by Hieron, No. 40 (E 93) and E 137. For one of the exterior scenes on No. 40 see Fig. 7. As regards subject, these vases illustrate the two tendencies of this artist—towards myth and legend on the one hand, and towards musical or conversation groups on the other. Together with this revival of myth and legend, which had been a conspicuous feature in the old black figure epoch, we see also in Hieron a return to the habit of inscribing on the vase the names of the mythical or legendary persons represented on it. And this is the more interesting when we observe how slight the difference sometimes is between an ordinary "conversation" scene and a mythical incident. On

in perfecting a type of face is rightly entitled to adhere to it in his day and generation.

As an unsigned work of Hieron we may fairly class No. 41 (E 22). At first sight the interior, with its precision of drawing and simplicity of composition, is suggestive of Duris. But the exterior speaks decisively for Hieron, with its "conversation" groups of figures in his large broad style, with bearded men, massive in build, inclining their heads sentimentally to smell a flower, or even without such a motive. We would also add No. 50 (E 74), with the interior group of a winged figure (Eos) pursuing a tall thin youth (Tithonos), which closely resembles a group on a vase signed by Hieron (Vorlegeblätter, ser. c, pl. 2). In this instance the exterior groups, though less strikingly in his manner, may yet not unfairly be assigned to him.

At the same time we must remember that of late a vase expressly signed by Hieron has been claimed, in spite of his signature, as the work of a

Fig. 7.

such a vase as our Fig. 8 the principal figure, Triptolemus, is easily recognised from his winged car; but, as regards the other figures, they are only distinguishable by their attributes as deities—without these and without inscribed names they would be ordinary figures; from which circumstance we see how the artists, in the interval of uninscribed scenes from daily life, had kept rigorously to a high, idealised level, so that no essential change was necessary when they came to substitute scenes of myth and legend.

In his heads Hieron is noticeable for a strongly marked type, with its massive chin and jaw and a comparatively short upper part of the face, the whole type being of a singularly large and simple mould. We have seen this type developing in Duris. It has now reached its highest point, and if it appears to be too constantly repeated, we must remember that an artist who thus succeeds

painter who does not give his name, but is assumed to have marked his individuality by a favour for figures of bald-headed old men (Hartwig, pl. 39, fig. 2, and pl. 40). We are asked to accept also as the work of this unidentified painter our No. 53 (E 37) and No. 52 (E 71), both of which contain in the interior a bald-headed man in conversation with another figure. But the designs on these two vases, both exterior and interior, differ very considerably in style, whereas what we would expect of this supposed co-worker of Hieron would be uniformity of style. The mere choice of bald-headed figures is not itself enough. One would rather fall back on Hieron himself and allow him some margin for differences of style, or failing that, assume that he had at times obtained the assistance of various painters, as we have seen he did in the case of Macron. We are inclined to ascribe No. 52 (E 71) directly to Hieron. The bald-headed old man in No. 44 (E 78) belongs to another category. We shall see that this vase probably was the work of Brygos, to whom we now proceed.

BRYGOS. — Comparatively few signed vases of this painter are known (eight altogether). The Museum possesses but one, No. 43 (E 77). It is, however, an excellent specimen and in most respects an adequate illustration of his style. The interior group consists of a seated warrior, to whom a female figure offers an oblation. On the exterior we have two scenes which appear to be drawn from the Satyric drama. The names of the characters are inscribed, and details are sometimes raised in relief and gilt; which facts, though not altogether unexampled till now, seem clearly to indicate a commencement of the stage of vase painting which was to follow, with its frequency of details so treated and its general omission of painters' names. Brygos may be regarded as a link between the two stages, and in fact he may

standing that the vase presents an artistic feature which we have not yet met with. That is to say, the deities on the exterior of the vase are represented of colossal proportions, while the Satyrs beside them are diminutive and drawn with minute precision. The effect in some measure reminds us of the difference of scale between the seated deities in the east frieze of the Parthenon and the standing figures beside them.

Another kylix of the same peculiar shape as these two, and of the same artistic manner, on the whole, is No. 45 (E 36), especially in the exterior scenes. But the interior group also contains a characteristic figure, that of a girl standing beside a column and holding up a vase. No. 47 (E 24) has been assigned to Brygos, and certainly the exterior groups recall his manner, not only in the spotted drapery, but also in the heads of the younger figures. He has a way of indicating the nostril by a finely curving line, which he seems to have developed from some examples of Euphronios, the

Fig. 8.

be said to have done much to create the new method. There is no denying that he still retains marked features of archaism. These he carried on from the school in which he had been trained. But the time had come when it was necessary to sacrifice some of the stateliness and grace of Hieron and Macron, and to infuse into his figures and his compositions something of the directness of actual life. Not that he goes far in this direction. It would hardly be true to say more than that this direct observation of life colours his work.

On the exterior of No. 43 (E 77) is a group of Satyrs rushing after Hera, which has been much and deservedly praised for its composition and drawing. Among the Satyrs is one in a most singular, crouching attitude, with very clever foreshortening. It happens that on the exterior of No. 44 (E 78) an almost identical Satyr occurs. So close is the resemblance and so peculiar the motive that we cannot hesitate to assign this vase also to Brygos, notwith-

effect being, in conjunction with the shortness of the nose, to give animation to the face. The exterior of this vase is also remarkable for the fine combination of nude forms against drapery, a combination which we have already noticed in Duris. It is known also in the work of Hieron. The peculiarly animated type of youthful heads in the work of Brygos is seen again in the exterior of No. 44 (E 65), with its somewhat violent domestic scenes, among which is an instance of a foreshortened figure which, in its boldness and coarseness, may well have been derived from Euphronios. The flute-player in the interior has a simple, somewhat archaic look, but that would not be sufficient evidence on which to class this vase as an early work of Brygos, considering the freedom and beauty of the exterior. No. 48 (E 27) has also been assigned to him; but if that is right, we must here recognize much of the influence of Hieron.

One of the most interesting of the unsigned vases which have been ascribed to Brygos is No. 49

(E 47), having in the interior a convivial scene of a girl dancing before a youth on a couch, and inscribed with the names of Philippos and Callisto.* The spelling "Pilipos" is supposed to indicate that Brygos was a Macedonian by birth, as indeed his name implies (see Hartwig, Meisterschalen, p. 319). It has been pointed out also that the youthfulness of the girl dancer is something new in Greek vase painting (Hartwig, p. 321). It undoubtedly goes well together with the youthful ness and animation of many of the figures of Brygos. But the girl is not only youthful, she is greatly in earnest; and this is perhaps one of the most marked characteristics of Brygos—the infusion of earnestness and animation into his figures, with a corresponding abandonment of the old stateliness and formality which Euphronios alone had fully broken through before him. The exterior scene of this vase, shown in Fig. 9, is finely composed, the figure of a youth leaning against a column is beautifully conceived and drawn, the whole scene is rich with detail and expressive in action, yet full of refinement and grace.

A. S. MURRAY.

* Some prefer to read εὔλλατος[?] as an epithet of Philippos.

Fig. 9.

17

DESCRIPTION OF PLATE I.

No. 1 (E 4). Signed by Thypheithides, ΕΠΟΙΕ̣SΕΝΕΥΦΕΙΘΙΔΕS. Subject, doe springing forward with head thrown back : around, ὁ παῖς καλός. Black on red.

Exterior, on each side a pair of large eyes as decoration, with a petal of anthemion between them.

Published, Klein, *Meisters.*[*] p. 97.

No. 2 (E 6). In the style of Thypheithides. Subject, a wreathed athlete bending to lift jumping weights (*haltères*) from the ground : around, ὁ παῖς καλός.

On the foot is engraved ΚΑΚΑΖΑΝΟΣ, in letters apparently of the VIth century B.C. This word suggests no known Greek name, and probably belongs to the category of unexplained graffiti on the feet of vases, which may be notes of the ancient seller, roughly scratched on in the shop. On the other hand, see the Memnon kylix in Munich (1087), which has the name ΚΑΚΑS.

Exterior, two scenes, each between large eyes : (1) A tall thin athlete stooping as if to pick up something. (2) A sepulchral stele (?) or a goal-post (?).

See Klein, *Euphronios,*[*] p. 298.

No. 3 (E 5). Signed by Hischylos ("made") and Pheidippos ("painted"), ΣΟΛΥ+ΣΙΗ ΕΠΟΙΕSΕΝ, ΦΕΙΔΙΠΟS ΕΛΡΑΦΕ. Subject, a Persian archer shooting an arrow.

Exterior, two scenes : (1) Between large eyes, a warrior running at full speed. (2) A scene in the palaestra ; dispute between a tall thin athlete and a short stout one ; another athlete throwing the javelin ; and a fourth poising the diskos, preparing to throw it.

Published, Klein, *Meistersig.*[*] p. 99.

No. 4 (E 21). In the style of Panphaeos. Subject, a warrior running, directing his spear against a pursuer, who is not shown.

Exterior, two scenes of warriors in combat. One of the warriors has his shield inscribed ΗΙΠΠΟΝ | ΙΠΠΟΛΛ ΙππΘΘ καλός. Cf. Klein, *Lieblingsinschr.* p. 73.

18

DESCRIPTION OF PLATE II.

No. 5 (E 16). In the style of Panphæos. Subject, a boy, wreathed, running with a joint of meat and a lyre; the inscription in the field is merely decorative.

Exterior, two scenes: (1) Combat of Heracles (supported by Athene) with Kyknos (supported by his father, Ares). (2) Combat of Dionysos with a giant (?); the horse and warrior on either side are probably added as decoration.

No. 6 (E 20). In the style of Panphæos. Subject, a man carrying a drinking-horn and a mantle. Inscribed ΚΑΛΟΣ ΦΕΙΔΟΝ.

The *exterior* scenes are each painted between two winged sea-horses. (1) Peleus seizes Thetis on the sea shore amidst her attendant Nereids. (2) Hermes and Nereids bring the news to the sea-god Nereus.

Engraved and published, Gerhard, *A. V.* III. pls. 178, 179. *Cf.* Klein, *Lieblingsinschr.* p. 36.

No. 7 (E 19). In the style of Panphæos. Subject, a Sphinx seated; in field, ὁ παῖς καλός.

Exterior, two scenes: (1) Achilles pursuing Troilos, who is on horseback, and a youthful runner inscribed as Telephos. (2) Three warriors charging, one of them on horseback; over them is inscribed ΗΕ+ΤΟΡ. Around one handle is painted a fortified wall (of Troy), with a doorway (the Skaian gate?); beneath the other handle, two warriors playing dice beside two willow trees.

Engraved and published, Gerhard, *A. V.* III. pl. 186; for the difficulties of interpretation, *cf.* Overbeck, *Her. Bildw.* p. 356.

No. 8 (E 9). Signed by Panphæos, ΠΑΝΦΑΙΟΣ ΕΠΟΙΕΣΕΝ. Subject, warrior charging.

The *exterior* scenes, each painted between two winged horses, placed decoratively, represent Dionysos, a Mænad playing castanets, and Seileni. The letters scattered over the field of the vase have no meaning.

Engraved and published, *Wiener Vorlegebl.* D. pl. 4; Klein, *Meistersig.* p. 94, No. 18.

Plate 11.

19

DESCRIPTION OF PLATE III.

No. 9 (E 10). Signed round the foot by Pamphæos, ΑΝΘΑΙΟΣ ΕΠΟΗΣΕΝ. Subject, Seilenos dancing.

On the *exterior*, two scenes: (1) Dead body of a man, lifted by two winged warriors (see Fig. 1, p. 7, *ante*). This subject, which is evidently mythological, recalls the Homeric legend of Sleep and Death bearing off the body of Sarpedon to a tomb in Lycia (*cf.* the lekythi, D 50 and D 54, on Case F). (2) Amazons arming. It has been thought that these scenes may have been the work of Euphronios.

Engraved and published, *Wiener Vorlegebl.* D, pl. 3. Klein, *Meistersig.'* p. 94, No. 20.

No. 10 (E 18). In the style of Pamphæos. Subject, Eros flying with a pomegranate. Inscribed twice καλός.

Exterior, two scenes from the Trojan War: (1) Troilos and Polyxena, having been to fetch water at a fountain outside the city, are pursued by Achilles. (2) The ὅπλων κρίσις, the quarrel of Ajax and Odysseus over the armour of Achilles; the disputants, rushing at one another, are restrained each by two young Greeks.

Birch, *Archæologia*, XXXII., pl. 10, gives (2). *Cf.* Robert, *Bild u. Lied*, p. 214.

No. 11 (E 11). In the style of Pamphæos. Subject, a girl with castanets dancing.

The *exterior* scenes are each painted between two Sirens playing flutes, placed decoratively, and represent Dionysos among his following, Seileni with thyrsos, wine-skin, &c., and a Mænad.

No. 12 (E 35). In the style of Chachrylion. Inscribed MEMNON ΚΑΛΟΣ. Subject, a nude youth bending forward, lifting a hydria.

The *exterior* scenes represent: (1) Departure of a warrior (inscribed " Ajax ") in a quadriga. (2) Dionysos among Seileni and Mænads.

Klein, *Meistersig.'* p. 120, No. 12. *Lieblingsnamen*, p. 34, No. 18.

Plate III.

20

DESCRIPTION OF PLATE IV.

No. 13 (E 31). In the style of Chelys or Chachrylion. Inscribed MEMNON KALOS. Subject, a nude youth, wreathed, stepping forward with a jug in his hand.

The *exterior* scenes have been described. Klein, *Lieblingsinschr.* p. 33, No. 15: they represent combats of warriors and Amazons. *Cf.* his *Meistersig.* p. 120, No. 10.

No. 14 (E 32). In the style of Chelys or Chachrylion. Inscribed MEMNON KALOS. Subject, a nude woman wearing a coif, stooping forward to attach her sandal.

Exterior, two scenes: (1) Heracles fighting with two Amazons. (2) Two youths dancing to the music of a bearded man, inscribed "Anacreon."

Engraved, Jahn, *Dichter auf Vasenb.* Taf. III. *Cf.* Klein, *Meistersig.* p. 122, No. 17.

No. 15 (E 31). In the style of Chachrylion (?). Inscribed MEMNON KALOS. Subject, an archer, crouching to shoot.

The *exterior* scenes have been engraved, Jahn, *Dichter auf Vasenb.* Taf. VI. *Cf.* Klein, *Euphronios,* p. 303: and *Meistersig.* p. 119, No. 7. They represent: (1) Revels of three youths. (2) A bearded man (inscribed 'Thalinos') playing the lyre to two other men (inscribed Xanthos and Molpis).

No. 16 (E 29). In the style of Euergides (?). Subject, a youth, wreathed, dancing in a bent attitude, holding a mantle on his arm.

The *exterior* has on one side the combat of Menelaos with a warrior, possibly Paris (?); on the other, a boy (perhaps Troilos ?) with two horses; over the boy is inscribed Πλήξιππος.

Cf. Archaeologia XXIII. p. 251, and XXXI. p. 265.

Plate IV

21

DESCRIPTION OF PLATE V.

No. 17 (E. 30). In the style of Panphæos (?). Subject, a youth wreathed, running; with inscription, ὁ παῖς καλός.

The *exterior* has on one side a youth running, leading two prancing horses; inscribed 'Hippocritos.' The other side seems to have been painted with a similar scene, which is now almost wholly destroyed.

Cf. Klein, *Lieblingsinschr.* p. 26.

No. 18 (E 33). In the style of Epictetos. Subject, a youth wearing helmet, shield and greaves, running and looking back; he has neither spear nor sword, and is probably a runner in the armed foot-race, hoplitodromos.

The same subject, probably, is shown on one of the *exterior* sides, where several youths are making preparations for the race: on the opposite side four warriors are running with spears shouldered.

Cf. the very similar series of scenes on the cup published by Gerhard, *A. V.* IV. pl. 261.

No. 19 (E 52). In the style of Epictetos: signed ΕΠΟΙΕΣΕΝ. Subject, a warrior with bow, looking along an arrow. For this motive, see Hartwig, *Meisterb.* p. 121, note 2.

Exterior, two scenes: (1) A battle-scene in which four warriors are engaged over the corpse of a fifth. (2) Revels of seven men.

Described, Klein, *Meistersig.* p. 112, No. 8.

No. 20 (E 12). In the style of Panphæos. Subject, a warrior with his horse.

Exterior, two scenes: (1) Combat of warriors with Pegasi and with other warriors. (2) Revels of Seileni. The letters in the field have no meaning; compare No. 8.

Described, Klein, *Meistersig.* p. 89.

Plate V.

17

18

19

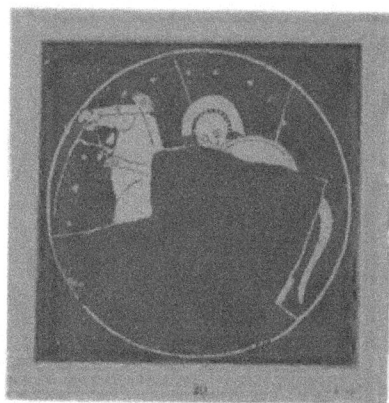

20

22

DESCRIPTION OF PLATE VI.

No. 21 (E 13). In the style of Epictetos. Subject, a youth wreathed, walking, with drinking-horn and staff.

Exterior, five scenes from the Labours of Theseus: (1) Capturing the Cretan bull. (2) Killing the sow of Crommyon in the presence of Hermes (the animal is represented, by an oversight of the artist, as a boar). (3) Killing Procrustes with his axe. (4) Wrestling with Kerkyon. (5) Killing the Minotaur.

Cf. Klein, *Euphronios*,' p. 196 (c).

No. 22 (E 8). Signed by Epictetos, ΕΠΙΚΤΕΤΟΣ ΕΛΡΑ.. ΕΝ. Subject, a man reclining on a couch, singing, and playing on the lyre. Above hangs a flute-case (sybene). Inscribed Ἱππαρ[χ]ο[ς] καλ[ός].

Exterior, two scenes: (1) Theseus slaying the Minotaur; on each side a maiden. (2) Revel of five youths.

Published, Klein, *Meistersig.*' p. 103, No. 9

No. 23 (E 7). Signed by Python ("made") and Epictetos ("painted"), ΠΥΘΟΝ ΕΠΟΙΕΣΕΝ, ΕΠΙΚΤΕΤΟΣ ΕΡΡΑΦΣΕ. Subject, a youth playing flutes and a girl dancing with castanets.

Exterior, two scenes: (1) Heracles slaying Busiris at altar amid his Egyptian priests and followers, see Fig. 2, p. 8, *ante*. (2) Symposium with music.

Published and engraved, Micali, *Stor. Ant* pl. 90, 1. Klein, *Meistersig.*' p. 103, No. 8.

No. 24 (E 44). Signed by Duris, ΔΟΡΙΣ .. ΡΑΦΣΕΝ. Subject, a youth with a sling in his left hand bending down to place something on an altar; inscribed with a favourite name of Duris, ΧΑΙΡΕΣΤRΑΤΟΣ ΙΚΑΛΟΣ.

The *exterior* scenes have been engraved, *Wiener Vorlegebl.* VIII. pl. 1., and represent groups of boxers with trainers, and youths with slings or boxing thongs.

Klein, *Meistersig.*' p. 152, No. 1; *Lieblingsinschr.* p. 52.

Plate VI.

23

DESCRIPTION OF PLATE VII.

No. 25 (E 15). Signed by Chachrylion, **Μ.ϛΗΟΤΥ .ΟΙΛVϞ+Α+**. Subject, an Amazon, fully armed, charging with spear couched.

The *exterior* scenes have been engraved in *Wiener Vorlegebl.* D. pl. 7. They represent: (1) Dionysos with dancing Seilenus and Mænad. (2) Revellers.

Klein, *Meistersig.* p. 126, No. 6.

No. 26 (E 14). Signed by Chachrylion, **ΚΟΙΛV+Α+** (*sic*); the *ἐποίησεν* is wanting. Subject, a youth playing on a cithara, and a girl with a flower: possibly the first meeting of Theseus and Ariadne, such as Pausanias saw on the chest of Kypselos—"Theseus holding a lyre, and near him Ariadne holding a crown (here it is a flower) in her hand" (Paus. v. 19, 1).

The *exterior* scenes have been engraved in *Wiener Vorlegebl.* D. pl. 7, and elsewhere. One side represents Theseus carrying off in a chariot Antiope, the queen of the Amazons, in the presence of Phorbas and Peirithoös; see Fig. 3, p. 9. *ante*; the other side, a youth and a girl conversing, and two boys on horseback.

Klein, *Meistersig.* p. 127, No. 8.

No. 27 (E 28). Signed by Euphronios, **EVϜΡΟΝΙΟϛ EΠΟΙΕϛEN**. Subject, a bearded man seated; before him stands a girl fastening or unfastening her girdle, at her feet a lyre; inscribed **ΠΑΝΑΙΤΙΟϛ ΚΑΛΟϛ**.

The *exterior* scenes are engraved in *Wiener Vorlegebl.* v. pl. 7. On one side Heracles brings the Erymanthian boar on his shoulders to Eurystheus, who has in terror got into a half-buried pithos; a woman and an old man hasten towards them; see Fig. 4. p. 10, *ante*. On the reverse, a quadriga driven by a young charioteer, from which a warrior has descended: in front of the chariot is Hermes.

Klein, *Meistersig.* p. 139, No. 4.

No. 28 (E 51). Ascribed to Euphronios (see p. 11, *ante*). Subject, two Amazons, Hippolyte and Thero, armed as hoplite and archer, charging.

A similar subject occurs on one of the exterior sides; on the other side is Heracles in combat with Amazons, and slaying with his club their queen Andromache, whom he has overthrown; see Fig. 5, p. 11, *ante*.

Engraved, Hartwig, *Meistersch.* pl. XIII. p. 118.

26   K 14   28   K 51

24

DESCRIPTION OF PLATE VIII.

No. 29 (E 49). Signed by Duris, ΔΟΡΙΣ ΕΓΡΑΦ·ΕΝ. Subject, Theseus slaying the Minotaur in Crete.

The *exterior* scenes have been engraved and published in *Wiener Vorlegebl.* vi. pl. 3; they represent the following labours of Theseus: (1) Casting the robber Skiron from the cliff, the goddess Athene looking on. At the foot of the cliff are the basin in which Skiron used to compel travellers to wash his feet, and the tortoise which devoured the travellers when they were cast over the cliff into the sea. (2) Wrestling with Kerkyon at Eleusis. For these two groups, see Fig. 6, p. 13, *ante*. (3) Attacking the sow of Crommyon, which an old woman, a personification of the locality, defends. (4) Dragging the robber Sinis to fasten him to the pine-tree, as he had been wont to fasten passing travellers.

Klein, *Meistersig.*[2] p. 158, No. 16.

No. 30 (E 48). Signed by Duris, ΔΟΡΙΣ ΕΓΡΑΦΣΕΝ (*sic*). Subject, a bearded man moving along, holding a staff and a cup in his hands and looking back.

The *exterior* scenes are engraved in *Wiener Vorlegebl.* vi. pl. 10. They represent symposia of men reclining on couches and drinking, attended by boys.

Klein, *Meistersig.*[2] p. 154, No. 7.

No. 31 (E 39). In the style of Duris. Subject, a girl closely draped, wearing a richly embroidered cap, raising a flower to her face and inhaling the scent. In the background is part of a bed, a basket, and a mirror hanging up. Inscribed, ἡ παῖς καλός (*sic*).

On the *exterior*, bearded figures and youths (some holding purses) conversing with women, probably hetæræ; from their gestures they seem to be bargaining.

Hartwig, *Meistersch.* p. 620, No. 2.

No. 32 (E 38). In the style of Duris. Subject, a bearded figure standing leaning on his staff: in the field hang a net (purse ?), a sponge, and an oil flask (?). Inscribed, ὁ παῖς καλός.

The *exterior* scenes represent groups of youths, mostly draped, leaning on staves, conversing with two bearded men, holding flowers; one youth, who is undraped, but decorated with ribands on his arm and head, is receiving a head-dress from a companion. These scenes probably take place in the palæstra or gymnasium.

Hartwig, *Meistersch.* p. 620. No. 3.

Plate VIII.

25

DESCRIPTION OF PLATE IX.

No. 33 (E 41). In the style of Duris. Subject, a draped bearded man holding a staff, seated before an altar, on which he pours a libation from a phialè; in the background are a kylix and a net purse, sponge and oil flask. Inscribed, ὁ παῖς καλός.

The *exterior* scenes represent bearded men with vases, dancing and singing; each wears the woollen fillet tied round the head to prevent intoxication (see Smith's *Dict. Ant.*[1] i. p. 550 *b*).

Hartwig, *Meistersch.* p. 622, No. 9.

No. 34 (E 40). In the style of Duris. Subject, two bearded men going to a banquet: one with a staff steadies his companion, who holds a jug and drinking vessel. Inscribed, ὁ παῖς καλός.

The *exterior* scenes show ten bearded men standing conversing, with drinking cups and vessels in hand, preparatory to the beginning of the banquet.

Hartwig, *Meistersch.* p. 622, No. 10.

No. 35 (E 42). In the style of Duris. Subject, a Mænad with thyrsos and wine jug.

The *exterior* scenes represent Dionysiac subjects: Dionysos holding vine and cantharos among Satyrs and Mænads.

Hartwig, *Meistersch.* p. 623, No. 11.

No. 36 (E 43). In the style of Duris. Subject, Odysseus announcing to Achilles that he is come to take away Briseis. Achilles is seated in an attitude of dejection, his head enveloped in his mantle; in the background hangs his sword and shield. Inscribed, ὁ παῖς καλός.

The *exterior* scenes are engraved in *Wiener Vorlegebl.* C. pl. 3, and represent a procession of women and warriors, and six other figures of men and youths conversing.

Hartwig, *Meistersch.* p. 600, note; p. 621, No. 6.

Plate IX.

26

DESCRIPTION OF PLATE X.

No. 37 (E 62). In the style of Duris. Subject, Hermes bearded, caduceus in right hand, lyre in left, flies over a wavy surface, probably representing the sea.

The *exterior* scenes are engraved in the *Mon. dell' Inst. Arch.* iv. pl. 33; they include scenes in the palæstra. In each case one youth, draped and wreathed, stands for the paido-tribes, and three other nude youths represent, by the objects held in their hands, jumping, disk throwing, and hurling the javelin.

No. 38 (E 64). In the style of Duris. Subject, a youth partially draped, walking and holding in his right hand a hare by the ears.

The *exterior* scenes represent draped ephebi, on one side listening to one of their number who is playing the flutes, on the reverse conversing with one who is seated holding a wreath.

No. 39 (E 45). In the style of Onesimos. Subject, a boy riding on a horse beside a tree; possibly an excerpt from a scene of Achilles and Troïlos [*cf.* No. 7].

The *exterior* scenes represent: (1) A bearded man and a youth arming in the presence of an old man and woman and two youths. (2) A combat in which seven warriors are engaged.

No. 40 (E 23). Signed by Hieron, ΗΙΕΡΟΝ ΕΠΟΙΕΣΕΝ. This inscription is incised on one handle. Subject, a girl dancing with castanets in the presence of a youth who is seated playing the flutes.

The *exterior* scenes are engraved in the *Wiener Vorlegebl.* C. pl. 5. They represent groups of men and youths conversing with hetæræ and flute-playing girls; see Fig. 7, p. 14, *ante*.

Klein, *Meisterng.* p. 165, No. 6.

27

DESCRIPTION OF PLATE XI.

No. 41 (E 22). In the style of Hieron. Subject, a bearded man seated, leaning on a staff, to whom a boy offers the leg of an animal and a dish of meats.

The *exterior* scenes take place in the gymnasium, as the strigil and sponge hanging up seem to show. The groups consist of bearded men and youths conversing. One of the bearded men holds a hare, as frequently occurs in similar scenes.

Hartwig, *Meistersch.* p. 295, No. 7.

No. 42 (E 26). In the style of Euphronios. Subject, Apollo pursuing a girl, possibly Daphne, though nothing is shown to suggest her transformation into a laurel. This scene is described in *Annali dell' Inst. Arch.* 1839, p. 251, as Apollo and Boline (Pausanias, vii. 23, 3).

The *exterior* scenes have been engraved in *Mon. dell' Inst. Arch.* iii. pl. 12; they represent a drinking bout of bearded men waited on by a boy with a jug; one sings with head thrown back to the music of lyre and flutes played by his companions. Below these scenes is a narrow band of boots, or vases in the form of boots, and drinking vessels, as in No. 48, *infra.*

Cf. the very similar vase published, *Philologus*, vol. 26, pl. iv., 1, which is assigned to Brygos by Hartwig, *Meistersch.* p. 105, note 1, 8.

No. 43 (E 77). Signed around the foot by Brygos, ΒΡΥΓΟΣ ΕΠΟΙΕΣΕΝ. Subject, a woman bringing wine to a seated warrior, who has apparently just returned and has handed her his shield. Inscribed with names 'Chrysippos' and 'Zeuxo.'

The *exterior* scenes have been engraved in *Wiener Vorlegebl.* viii. pl. 6, and elsewhere. They represent: (1) Iris holding a curved object, resembling an oxtail (*cf.* the vase in Berlin, Cat. 2591, which has the same subject), attacked by three Seileni at an altar near which Dionysos stands; a scene probably borrowed from the Satyric drama: (2) Hera, set upon by four Seileni, is succoured by Hermes and Heracles.

Klein, *Meistersig.* p. 183, No. 8.

No. 44 (E 78). In the style of Brygos. Subject, an elderly bearded figure standing beside a folding stool.

The *exterior* scenes represent Dionysos and Heracles at a banquet, attended by Seileni; and Dionysos reclining alone with a drinking cup, and two Seileni, one of whom dances, while the other plays the flutes. On the left are a mixing bowl and jug.

Hartwig, *Meistersch.* p. 443, note 1.

28

DESCRIPTION OF PLATE XII.

No. 45 (E. 36). In the style of Brygos. Subject, a girl pouring wine for a bearded man, who is seated on a chair; in the background is seen part of a building.

The *exterior* scenes are engraved in Gerhard, *Trinksch.* i. pl. D. They represent: (1) Zeus(?) and Hera(?), attended by a youth (Ganymede?) and Iris(?); in the centre is Ares, fully armed. (2) Memnon overthrown in combat by Achilles; on either side Thetis and Eos, the mothers of the combatants, rush forward. Below one handle, a panther.

Hartwig, *Meistersch.* p. 361.

No. 46 (T. 47). In the style of Brygos. Inscribed, ΡΙΡΟΝ ΚΑΛΟΣ (*sic*). Subject, a youth reclining at a banquet, holding flutes and signing to a girl who dances before him, raising with both hands her skirt.

The *exterior* scenes represent symposia, in which on each side a bearded man and a young man are occupied with hetaerae and musicians; see Fig. 9, p. 16, *ante*.

Engraved in Hartwig, *Meistersch.* pl. xxxiv., *cf.* Klein, *Lieblingsinschr.* p. 61.

No. 47 (E. 24). In the style of Brygos. Subject, Paris leading away Helen; Paris wears the dress of a traveller, Helen that of a bride.

The *exterior* scenes represent, on the one side, Ajax and Odysseus, who have quarrelled over the arms of Achilles (shown under the handles of the vase), and who rush at each other, but are restrained by Greeks: on the other, Greeks deciding the quarrel by vote in the presence of Athene. This scene is almost identical with one signed by Duris (*Mon. dell' Inst. Arch.* viii. pl. 41). On the right stands Ajax in a dejected attitude, with the fewer votes on his side: on the left is Odysseus, who is successful.

Engraved in *Archaeologia*, xxxix. pls. 9, 11, and elsewhere.

No. 48 (E. 27). In the style of Brygos. Subject, two youths at a banquet, waited on by a boy.

The *exterior* scenes have been described by Jahn in *Philologus*, 26, p. 228, and are two scenes of symposium, with eight youths and two bearded men reclining on couches and drinking; below these scenes is a narrow band, on which are painted pairs of boots, or vases in form of boots, and various drinking vessels.

Hartwig, *Meistersch.* p. 330.

Plate XII.

29

DESCRIPTION OF PLATE XIII.

No. 49 (E 63). In the style of Brygos. Subject, a youth wreathed, dancing and playing on the flutes ; beside him his staff and a basket hanging up.

The *exterior* scenes are engraved in *Arch. Zeit.* 1870, pl. 39 ; they represent revelry, youths dancing to the sound of flutes played by a youth and a girl, and others on couches. Beneath one handle is a vase of unusual form inscribed "kalos." *

* *Cf.* the vase published in Fröhner, *Van Branteghem Collection*, pl. 28, No. 77 ("style of Brygos").

No. 50 (E 74). In the style of Brygos. Subject, Eos (the Dawn) pursuing Tithonos (or perhaps Kephalos), who is characterised by the lyre which he holds in his right hand. For Kephalos with lyre, see Robert, *Bild u. Lied*, p. 32, note 36.

The *exterior* scenes represent bearded men and youths conversing ; armour hanging up in the background.

No. 51 (E 73). In a rough style, possibly related to that of Hieron. Subject, a bearded man and a youth conversing.

The *exterior* scenes represent two of the labours of Theseus, viz. : (1) His punishment of Sinis, the pine-bender, by fastening the robber to the bent pine tree ; the tree released sprang back to a vertical position, and in this way the victims of Sinis met their death. (2) His combat with the sow of Crommyon ; the personification of the locality, an old dishevelled woman, stands by.

No. 52 (E 71). In the style of Hieron. Subject, a bald old man, wearing a fringed chiton, arrives at the door of a house before which stands a young man, whom he addresses.

The *exterior* scenes are engraved in Hartwig, *Meistersch.* pl. xliii. ; they represent Dionysos with Thracian boots, holding a snake and thyrsos, dancing in the midst of Seileni and Mænads, who also dance to the sound of pipes played by Seileni.

Plate XIII.

30

DESCRIPTION OF PLATE XIV.

No. 53 (E. 37). In the style of Hieron. Subject, a bald old man seated on a stool conversing with a bearded figure, both wreathed; possibly this represents some episode in the councils of the Greeks which preceded the events shown on the exterior.

The *exterior* scenes are published in Hartwig, *Meistersch.* pl. XLI. On one side the heralds are leaving Achilles, who sits mourning in his tent, with Briseis; on the reverse, they are leading off Briseis to restore her to her father.

No. 54 (E 70). Unassigned. Subject, a youth leaning on a staff in front of a woman seated in a chair, who holds up in her fingers two flowers (?); in the background, a mirror.

The *exterior* scenes represent: (1) The combat of Achilles and Memnon in the presence of Thetis and Eos, who rush forward, each towards her own champion. (2) A group of three warriors who approach a bearded man in a chlamys, holding a staff: this also may be an episode from the Iliad, connected with the anger of Achilles.

No. 55 (E. 46). In the style of Brygos (?). Subject, a boxer arming himself with boxing thongs, *himantes*; beside him a trainer with the forked rod used for the correction of youths in the palæstra.

The *exterior* scenes represent subjects from the palæstra. On one side, a contest of pancratiasts, and a trainer; part of this group is engraved in Hartwig, *Meistersch.* p. 392. On the other side, a runner in the armed foot-race, a trainer, a pair of boxers, and a jumper (?).

No. 56 (E 25). Unassigned. Subject, parting scene between youth and female figure, who offers him wine in a phialè.

The *exterior* has on one side a subject very similar to this; on the other, a procession of three men and a woman towards a man seated in a dejected attitude.

31

DESCRIPTION OF PLATE XV.

No. 57 (E 55). Later fine style. Subject, Cadmos, represented as a youthful figure with a hydria, receiving from Athene the stone wherewith to kill the serpent.

The *exterior* scenes, representing the destruction of the children of Niobe by Apollo on one side, and by Artemis on the other, are engraved and published in the *Berichte der sächs. Ges.* 1875, pl. 3, *a–c.*

No. 58 (E 56). Later fine style. Subject, two athletes at the bath, using the strigil (partly restored).

The *exterior* scenes are published and engraved in Gerhard, *A. V.* iv. pl. 277: they represent a continuation of the scene just described—groups of athletes at the bath. In one is a curious representation of a well, with cross-beam and bucket for lowering.

No. 59 (E 50). Unassigned. Subject, a pair of women, whose thyrsi bespeak them as Mænads, though their dress is that of ordinary Athenian women.

The *exterior* scenes represent pairs of figures, youths and men conversing with women, probably hetæræ, who hold objects of toilet use, such as dressing-case, mirror and oil-flask.

No. 60 (E 54). Later fine style. Subject, Pluto reclining on a couch, at the foot of which Persephone is seated; Pluto holds in one hand his emblem, the horn, in the other a drinking-cup.

The *exterior* scenes are engraved and published, *Mon. dell' Inst. Arch.* v. pl. 49. They represent the banquet of the gods, attended by Ganymedes and a Seilenos (Komos) as cupbearers: each god is accompanied by his consort, seated on the edge of his couch: there are present on one side, Zeus with Hera, Poseidon with Amphitrite; on the reverse, Dionysos with Ariadne, and Ares with Aphrodite.

No. 61 (E 112). Late style. Subject, a woman seated, to whom her attendant (?) brings a toilet-case, pyxis, sash, and wreath.

The *exterior* scenes represent: (1) Two women with wine-jug, phialè and box, advancing to Apollo (?), who holds a staff of laurel. (2) Two women bringing objects of toilet use to a woman who holds a sceptre.

No. 62 (E 72). Late style. Subject, Heracles and Nemean lion.

The *exterior* scenes represent two more of the labours of Heracles: on one side, his contest with the Cretan bull, in the presence of two other figures, one of whom is attired like Heracles: on the other, his carrying off the cattle of Geryon.

Hartwig, *Meisterisch.* p. 675, note 1.

Plate XV